A LIFEBUILDER  BI

THESSA   NS

How Can I   Jure?

*11 Studies
for individuals or groups*

Donald Baker

With Notes for Leaders

SCRIPTURE UNION
130 City Road, London EC1V 2NJ

Contents

Getting the Most
from LifeBuilder Bible Studies

Many of us long to fill our minds and our lives with Scripture. We desire to be transformed by its message. LifeBuilder Bible Studies are designed to be an exciting and challenging way to do just that. They help us to be guided by God's Word in every area of life.

How They Work

LifeBuilders have a number of distinctive features. Perhaps the most important is that they are *inductive* rather than *deductive*. In other words, they lead us to *discover* what the Bible says rather than simply *telling* us what it says.

They are also thought-provoking. They help us to think about the meaning of the passage so that we can truly understand what the author is saying. The questions require more than one-word answers.

The studies are personal. Questions expose us to the promises, assurances, exhortations and challenges of God's Word. They are designed to allow the Scriptures to renew our minds so that we can be transformed by the Spirit of God. This is the ultimate goal of all Bible study.

The studies are versatile. They are designed for student, neighborhood and church groups. They are also effective for individual study.

How They're Put Together

LifeBuilders also have a distinctive format. Each study need take no more than forty-five minutes in a group setting or thirty minutes in personal study – unless you choose to take more time.

The studies can be used within a quarter system in a church and fit well in a semester or trimester system on a college campus. If a guide has more than thirteen studies, it is divided into two or occasionally three parts of approximately twelve studies each.

LifeBuilders use a workbook format. Space is provided for writing answers to each question. This is ideal for personal study and allows group members to prepare in advance for the discussion.

The studies also contain leader's notes. They show how to lead a group discussion, provide additional background information on certain questions, give helpful tips on group dynamics and suggest ways to deal with problems which may arise during the discussion. With such helps, someone with little or no experience can lead an effective study.

Suggestions for Individual Study

1. As you begin each study, pray that God will help you to understand and apply the passage to your life.

2. Read and reread the assigned Bible passage to familiarize yourself with what the author is saying. In the case of book studies, you may want to read through the entire book prior to the first study. This will give you a helpful overview of its contents.

3. A good modern translation of the Bible, rather than the King James Version or a paraphrase, will give you the most help. The New International Version, the New American Standard Bible and the Revised Standard Version are all recommended. However, the questions in this guide are based on the New International Version.

4. Write your answers in the space provided in the study guide. This will help you to express your understanding of the passage clearly.

5. It might be good to have a Bible dictionary handy. Use it to look up any unfamiliar words, names or places.

Suggestions for Group Study

1. Come to the study prepared. Follow the suggestions for individual study mentioned above. You will find that careful preparation will greatly enrich your time spent in group discussion.

2. Be willing to participate in the discussion. The leader of your group will not be lecturing. Instead, he or she will be encouraging the members of the group to discuss what they have learned from the passage. The leader will be asking the questions that are found in this guide. Plan to share what God has taught you in your individual study.

3. Stick to the passage being studied. Your answers should be based on the verses which are the focus of the discussion and not on outside authorities such as commentaries or speakers. This guide deliberately avoids jumping from book to book or passage to passage. Each study focuses on only one passage. Book studies are generally designed to lead you through the book in the order in which it was written. This will help you follow the author's argument.

4. Be sensitive to the other members of the group. Listen attentively when they share what they have learned. You may be surprised by their insights! Link what you say to the comments of others so the group stays on the topic. Also, be affirming whenever you can. This will encourage some of the more hesitant members of the group to participate.

5. Be careful not to dominate the discussion. We are sometimes so eager to share what we have learned that we leave too little opportunity for others to respond. By all means participate! But allow others to also.

6. Expect God to teach you through the passage being discussed and through the other members of the group. Pray that you will have an enjoyable and profitable time together.

7. If you are the discussion leader, you will find additional suggestions and helpful ideas for each study in the leader's notes. These are found at the back of the guide.

Introducing 1 & 2 Thessalonians

Conventional wisdom tells us that nothing is certain except death and taxes, but for most of us that is not enough. Wouldn't you like to be just as sure about where you stand with God? That's what the Thessalonians were looking for, and Paul's letters to them can help you to find that assurance as well.

In the year A.D. 50, Paul entered Thessalonica while on his second missionary journey. He preached there for three weeks and was able to establish a church. However, a group of jealous Jews interpreted Paul's message to mean that he was proclaiming another ruler in opposition to the Roman emperor, and he was forced to leave town (Acts 17:1-10).

Because of Paul's concern for this young church, he sent his coworker, Timothy, to learn how the Thessalonians were doing. Timothy reported that the Christians' faith remained strong but that they continued to be persecuted by those who had banished Paul. Timothy also brought back questions which Paul had not had time to answer during his short stay with them.

First Thessalonians was Paul's first attempt at offering encouragement and answering questions—in fact it was probably the first of Paul's epistles. It was written from Corinth only a few months after Paul had left Thessalonica. Second Thessalonians was written a short time later to clear up misconceptions which the first letter had failed to answer.

In these letters, Paul offers encouragement in four major areas: (1) How can I be sure that I will be with Jesus after death? (2) How can I be sure that Jesus is coming again? (3) How can I be sure that Jesus hasn't forgotten me when I am suffering persecution? (4) How can I be sure that my life is pleasing to God?

Through your study of these letters, it is my hope that you will become sure of your faith and of your salvation and that, as a result, you will be able to "encourage each other with these words" (1 Thess 4:18).

1
Believers in a Hostile City

Acts 17:1-15

Standing up for the minority is never comfortable, but when the majority happens to be an angry mob, and you are expected to be the minority spokesperson, and you aren't sure you are ready to defend what you believe, then it becomes a nightmare. In this study we will meet a man in just such a predicament.

Perhaps you have felt yourself outnumbered by opponents or overwhelmed by a society that rejects your beliefs. If so, you will find yourself identifying with Jason and the other Christians in Thessalonica.

1. Have you ever had to defend your beliefs in front of people who disagreed? What did you say?

2. Read Acts 17:1-15. Why were the Thessalonian Jews so jealous of Paul (vv. 4-5)?

3. To what extent were the accusations made against the Christians a misunderstanding?

4. How should we, as Christians, react to jealousy and misunderstanding?

5. Imagine yourself as Jason (vv. 5-7). You have been a Christian about three weeks and must defend yourself and your houseguests before the city officials. How would you have felt in this position?

What would you have said?

6. Describe the Bereans' response in verses 11-12.

7. The Jews from Thessalonica make an appearance again (v. 13). How would you characterize the Bereans in comparison to the Thessalonians?

8. Sometimes Christians are accused of being closed-minded. What can the Thessalonians and Bereans teach you about being open-minded?

9. What challenges and discouragements would a Christian in Thessalonica have experienced?

10. If you had been Paul writing a letter to the Thessalonians, what would you have wanted to say to them?

11. When have you experienced challenges and discouragements similar to those of the Thessalonians?

12. In what ways can Christians encourage each other during such difficult times?

2
Faith
That Shows
1 Thessalonians 1:1-10

Alighthouse has become a common analogy for a church. Just as a lighthouse stands in a dark and dangerous spot flashing its message of warning and pointing to safe harbor, a church should also be a prominent and unmistakable sign to the community in which it exists. How can you help your church or fellowship group become such a shining light? This passage describes how the church in Thessalonica was able to do it.

1. What is the reputation of your church or fellowship group throughout the community?

2. Read 1 Thessalonians 1. What facts convinced Paul that the Thessalonians' faith was genuine (v. 3)?

3. Paul writes that he remembers the Thessalonians' "work produced by faith," "labor prompted by love," and "endurance inspired by hope"

(v. 3). How do you think he could tell that faith, love and hope were behind their actions?

4. Who do you know that has demonstrated this kind of faith?

How has the faith of these people inspired you?

5. What role has the Holy Spirit played in the Thessalonians' faith (vv. 5-6)?

6. How has the Holy Spirit brought conviction and joy to you?

7. What role did Paul, Silas and Timothy have in the Thessalonians' conversion (v. 6)?

8. When is it wise and when is it unwise to imitate another Christian (vv. 6-7)?

9. What were the results of the Thessalonians' strong faith (vv. 8-10)?

10. How can your faith (and the faith of your church or fellowship group) become more of a witness to others?

11. How would this chapter have been an encouragement to the Thessalonians?

How is it an encouragement to you?

3
Gentle Evangelism
1 Thessalonians 2:1-16

What thoughts come to your mind when you hear the word *evangelism?* Pushy people trying to get you to see things their way? Guilt for not saying enough about your Savior? People swarming down the aisles at a gigantic rally? Or friends sharing the excitement of good news with each other? For Paul, evangelism was always delightful and exciting. In this passage he tells us why talking about Christ is such a positive experience for him.

1. Has telling others about your faith been a positive or a negative experience? Explain.

2. Read 1 Thessalonians 2:1-6. What excuses might Paul have had not to preach to the Thessalonians (vv. 1-2)?

3. What attitudes enabled Paul to continue preaching despite opposition (vv. 3-6)?

4. What does this teach you about proper and improper reasons for witnessing to others?

5. Read 1 Thessalonians 2:7-16. How was Paul "like a mother caring for her little children" (vv. 7-9)?

6. In what specific ways can gentleness and caring become more a part of your evangelistic efforts?

7. Paul claims to have been "holy, righteous and blameless" (v. 10) among the Thessalonians. If this is important, how can imperfect people dare to do evangelism?

8. How is a father dealing with his children a good example of an evangelist (v. 11-12)?

9. What difficulties did the Thessalonians face in sharing their faith with others (vv. 14-16)?

10. What encouragement does Paul give them not to give up?

11. In what ways have you found evangelism to be difficult?

12. What ideas and encouragement from this passage can help you to overcome these difficulties?

4
Unmistakable Love

1 Thessalonians 2:17—3:13

Studies show that more people leave their churches today for lack of love than for any other reason.* It is indeed sad that even those who are committed to the Lord of love are unable to offer that love to others. How can your church become a place where love will "increase and overflow for each other and for everyone else" (1 Thess 3:12)? This passage provides some practical examples.

1. On a scale of 1-10, how loved do you feel by the members of your church or fellowship group?

Why did you give that ranking?

2. Read 1 Thessalonians 2:17—3:13. What evidence do you find in this passage that Paul really did love the Thessalonians (2:17, 20; 3:2, 5, 10)?

3. What phrases does Paul use to express his love (2:17-18; 3:5)?

4. How do you most often express your love for others?

What ideas from this passage can help you become even better at expressing love?

5. What fears caused Paul to send Timothy to Thessalonica (3:2-5)?

6. How had Paul prepared the Thessalonians for hardship (3:4)?

7. What further help do you think Timothy might have given during his visit?

8. How can you show love to people who are suffering?

9. Why was Timothy's report such good news to Paul (3:6-8)?

10. What are Paul's desires for the Thessalonians (3:10-13)?

How do these desires reflect Paul's love and caring?

11. How might Paul's example have helped the Thessalonians' love to "increase and overflow" (v. 12)?

---

12. How can you (as an individual or group) help love to increase within your church or fellowship group?

---

*Win Arn, Carroll Nyquist and Charles Arn, *Who Cares about Love?* (Pasadena, Calif.: Church Growth Press, 1986), p. 7.

5
A Life That Pleases God

1 Thessalonians 4:1-12

All of us want to please the people we love the most. That is why a wife will surprise her husband with his favorite meal, a husband will plan a special evening at a concert he knows will excite his wife, or a child will pick a bouquet of dandelions to present to Mom and Dad. What can Christians do to please God, whom they love so dearly? This passage offers some ideas.

---

1. If a Christian brother or sister asked you for advice on how to make their life more pleasing to God, what is the first thing you would say?

---

2. Read 1 Thessalonians 4:1-12. Why would Paul give these instructions on holy living to people whom he says are already living a life which pleases God (vv. 1, 10)?

3. Why is it important for us to keep reminding ourselves of how we ought to live (v. 3)?

4. What clues does this passage give as to how Paul would define sexual immorality (vv. 3-6)?

5. What reasons does Paul give for avoiding sexual immorality (vv. 5-8)?

6. How does sexual immorality "wrong" or "take advantage of" a brother (v. 6)?

7. How can this passage help you to resist sexual temptation?

8. In verses 9 and 10, Paul commends the Thessalonians for their love.

What could a group with such a reputation do to love each other even more?

How can these ideas be applied to your church or fellowship group?

9. Scholars agree that verses 11 and 12 were directed toward members of the church who had quit working and were relying on the kindness of their fellow Christians to provide them with necessities. Why would Paul have been concerned about the effect this attitude was having on outsiders?

10. What do unbelievers notice about your work habits which attracts them to Christ?

What work habits detract from your Christian witness?

11. Paul has given commands in this passage concerning sexual immorality, love for fellow Christians, and work. What can you do this week to become more obedient in one of these areas?

6
The Hope of Christ's Coming

1 Thessalonians 4:13—5:11

A crisis occurred in the Thessalonian church when one of their members died. Since they had expected to all be alive when Christ returned, they were now confused. Did this mean their friend would miss out on Christ's coming? Had this person died because God was angry with them? How much longer would it be before Christ finally did return?

Perhaps you have been wondering about similar questions. Maybe you have fears about what will happen when you die or when Christ returns. In this passage, Paul seeks to calm our fears and encourage us to look forward to the day we meet our maker.

1. What fears do you have about death?

2. Read 1 Thessalonians 4:13-18. In what ways is grief different for a Christian than it is for a non-believer (v. 13)?

3. What sequence of events does Paul say will occur when Christ returns (vv. 16-17)?

4. How would Paul's words have encouraged the Thessalonians?

How can they help you to face your own fears about death?

5. Read 1 Thessalonians 5:1-11. What is the "day of the Lord" (v. 2)?

6. Why are the examples of a thief (v. 2) and labor pains (v. 3) good analogies of what will happen on the day of the Lord?

7. What kinds of reactions can we expect to see from non-Christians when Christ returns (v. 3)?

How will Christians react (vv. 4-6)?

8. What dangers are associated with living in darkness (vv. 5-7)?

9. What instructions does Paul give for living in the light (v. 8)?

10. Paul tells us that our defensive weapons against darkness are faith, love and hope (v. 8). What are some practical ways in which these virtues can defend you?

11. What is God's plan for us (vv. 9-11)?

12. How can you prepare for the day of the Lord?

7
Life Among Friends
1 Thessalonians 5:12-28

Any group of people needs rules for getting along, and the church is no exception. Paul so wants the Thessalonians to "live in peace with each other" (1 Thess 5:13), that he closes his first letter to them with several instructions on how they can do this. These are instructions which have never gone out of date and can still be used to end the quarrels, hurt feelings and resentments in your church or fellowship group.

1. If you had the power to make one rule for helping people get along, what would it be?

2. Read 1 Thessalonians 5:12-28. What does it mean for someone to be "over you in the Lord" (v. 12)?

3. What could you do to show your regard for such a person in your church or fellowship?

4. The instructions Paul gives to all the "brothers" in verses 14-15 sound very much like the kind of things you would expect only a leader to do. What does·this teach you about the responsibilities of every member of the church?

5. How can you warn a person about something they are doing wrong (v. 14) or prevent them from taking revenge (v. 15) and still live in peace with them?

6. What does it mean to be joyful "always," pray "continually" and give thanks "in all circumstances" (vv. 16-18)?

7. Verses 19-22 teach about a Christian's relationship with the Holy Spirit. How might a person treat prophecy with contempt?

8. How can you test things like prophecy or teaching to find out if they are good or evil?

9. How can a greater openness to the Spirit improve human relationships within a group of Christians?

10. Look through the passage again, and pick out the actions and attitudes (stated or implied) which are displeasing to God. What are they?

11. What does God do to keep you from these sins (vv. 23-24)?

12. When have you found God faithful in keeping you from sin (v. 24)?

8
Evidence
of Faith
2 Thessalonians 1:1-12

Can I know for sure that I will go to heaven?

This is a question that plagued the Thessalonians to such an extent that even after the comfort of his first letter, Paul has to write again and give further encouragement. It was difficult for these young Christians to believe that the suffering of their present life would really be followed by the eternal joy of heaven.

Perhaps you also wonder if heaven really exists and if you can be sure of going there. If so, you will find Paul writing this passage directly to you.

1. Have you ever met a person and gone away thinking, "They must be a Christian." What gave you that impression?

2. Read 2 Thessalonians 1:1-12. What good things does Paul notice about the lives of the Thessalonians (vv. 3-4)?

3. Why do you think that in times of persecution, some people's faith and love grows while others' fails (v. 4)?

How can you make sure that yours is the kind that will grow?

4. What is the "evidence that God's judgment is right" (v. 5)?

5. "Suffering . . . is not to be thought of as evidence that God has forsaken us, but as evidence that God is with us."* How has God been evident in your times of suffering?

6. Paul proclaims that "God is just." How does he describe God's justice (vv. 6-10)?

7. How do you think suffering people like the Thessalonians would have responded to this teaching about God's justice?

8. How can God's justice encourage you when things are "just not fair"?

9. According to this passage, what makes a person "worthy of the kingdom" (v. 5) or "worthy of [God's] calling" (v. 11)?

10. What will cause God to punish some people when he returns (vv. 8-10)?

11. In light of his teaching about God's judgment, why does Paul pray as he does in verses 11-12?

12. If someone were to pray this prayer for you, what is one specific way in which you would want God to change your life?

---

*Leon Morris, *The First and Second Epistles to the Thessalonians,* New International Commentary on the New Testament (Grand Rapids: Eerdmans, 1959), p. 198.

9
Lawlessness on the Loose
2 Thessalonians 2:1-17

How will the world end? Will there be nuclear war? An evil empire? The destruction of civilization? Paul advises us that Satan has yet to attack us with the worst he has, and when he does, it will be a fearful time to be alive. However, Paul also promises that God will always be in control.

1. What potential threats to the safety of the world do you see right now (for example, attitudes, weapon-building, warfare and so on)?

2. Read 2 Thessalonians 2. In 1 Thessalonians 4:13-18 we saw how Paul responded to the fears of the Thessalonians that if they died before Christ returned, they would miss the joy Christ had for them. Apparently, after Paul sent the first letter, someone tried to convince the Thessalonians that the day of the Lord had already come. Considering the misconceptions they already had about Christ's return, how would this have affected them?

3. What is Paul's proof that the day of the Lord has not come (vv. 3, 9)?

4. What can you learn about the "man of lawlessness" from this passage (vv. 3-4, 7-10)?

5. Paul reminds the Thessalonians that he has already told them what is holding back the lawless one (vv. 5-6). Unfortunately, this was something he told them orally, and we don't know what he said. Despite the fact that this information is missing, what can be learned about the way God prevents his people from being destroyed?

6. In what ways have you noticed the "secret power of lawlessness" (v. 7) to be already at work?

7. Why will God cause people to believe the lies of the lawless one (v. 11)?

8. What contrasts do you find between those whom God condemns (vv. 10-12) and those whom he chooses for salvation (vv. 13-17)?

9. How can you be sure that you are a part of the group chosen for salvation?

10. Even for Christians, the lawless one will bring fear and testing. What can you do to prepare yourself to withstand him?

11. How can this passage encourage you about facing the future?

10
Lazy
Christians

2 Thessalonians 3:1-18

Members of the Thessalonian church were refusing to take responsibility. Some had quit working because they thought Jesus would be back any moment and didn't see any reason to exert themselves. Others relaxed because there were plenty of wealthier members in the church who were always willing to share. Regardless of the reason, Paul was abhorred by such laziness and set the rule, "If a man will not work, he shall not eat."

How can our laziness affect the work of Christ? What can we do about the laziness of others? Paul addresses those questions in this study.

1. In most churches, the majority of the work is done by a small minority of the people. Why do you think this is true?

2. Read 2 Thessalonians 3:1-5. In what ways did Paul expect that his ministry could be enhanced because of the Thessalonians' prayer (vv. 1-2)?

3. How is Paul's confidence in the Lord expressed in this request for prayer (vv. 3-5)?

4. What encouragement and ideas do these verses give you concerning your own prayer life?

5. Read 2 Thessalonians 3:6-18. How would you describe the problem the Thessalonian church was experiencing (v. 11)?

What effect do you imagine this was having on the church and the community?

6. In what ways do lazy Christians still continue to take advantage of the work of others?

What are the effects?

7. How did Paul make himself an example of the proper attitude toward work (vv. 7-9)?

8. How can you become a similar example to others?

9. What actions are to be taken against those who refuse to work (vv. 12-15)?

10. Why would this have been a good method of dealing with the problem in Thessalonica?

11. What principles for discipline that could be applied in the church today do you find in this passage?

11
Turning On the Power

1 & 2 Thessalonians

When learning to use a new piece of equipment, the instructions will first familiarize you with each of the controls and then teach you how to put them into operation. But when you have finally finished reading the directions, it is up to you to turn it on and make it work for your benefit.

So far our study of Thessalonians has been like reading the directions—it has taught us some things about the Christian faith and how they can be applied. It is now up to us to put these teachings into practice in our modern world.

1. What are the major themes Paul has emphasized in the letters to the Thessalonians?

2. Paul speaks about the Second Coming of Christ in both 1 Thessalonians 4:13—5:11 and 2 Thessalonians 2. How would you summarize his teaching?

3. What effect should knowledge about the Second Coming have on our daily living?

4. The future is a subject which has fascinated modern thinkers. How would Paul respond to the following reports?

In 1955, two days before Albert Einstein died, he and Bertrand Russell delivered a "Manifesto" in London. Describing the risks of thermonuclear war, they claimed, "We have found that the men who know most are the most gloomy." Russell's own view of the world was expressed in his poignant words: "Only on the firm foundation of unyielding despair can the soul's habitation be safely built."

In a BBC *Controversy* progamme in September 1973, the well-known "futurologist" Hermann Kahn presented the case for optimism. In a hundred years or so, he suggested, we could expect a world population of 15,000,000,000, with each family owning three houses, two cars and perhaps a submarine. He admitted that probably seventy major world problems would crop up in the next ten or twenty years, but "given moderately reasonable behaviour" the human race would survive to enjoy his projected utopia.*

5. A friend of yours becomes interested in reincarnation saying, "It helps me face death." She asks for your opinion. Using the teachings found in Thessalonians, how would you counsel her?

---

6. What principles have you learned about enduring times of suffering (1 Thess 1:2-7; 3:1-10)?

about sharing your faith with others (1 Thess 2)?

about pleasing God (1 Thess 4:1-12; 5:12-22; 2 Thess 3:6-15)?

about God's justice (2 Thess 1:3-10)?

7. What changes have you observed in your life as a result of studying Thessalonians?

8. What have you enjoyed most about studying these letters?

---

*Quotes taken from *The Jesus Hope* by Stephen Travis (Downers Grove, Ill.: InterVarsity Press, 1974), pp. 16-17.

Leader's Notes

Leading a Bible discussion can be an enjoyable and rewarding experience. But it can also be *scary*—especially if you've never done it before. If this is your feeling, you're in good company. When God asked Moses to lead the Israelites out of Egypt, he replied, "O Lord, please send someone else to do it!" (Ex 4:13).

When Solomon became king of Israel, he felt the task was far beyond his abilities. "I am only a little child and do not know how to carry out my duties. . . . Who is able to govern this great people of yours?" (1 Kings 3:7, 9).

When God called Jeremiah to be a prophet, he replied, "Ah, Sovereign LORD, . . . I do not know how to speak; I am only a child" (Jer 1:6).

The list goes on. The apostles were "unschooled, ordinary men" (Acts 4:13). Timothy was young, frail and frightened. Paul's "thorn in the flesh" made him feel weak. But God's response to all of his servants—including you—is essentially the same: "My grace is sufficient for you" (2 Cor 12:9). Relax. God helped these people in spite of their weaknesses, and he can help you in spite of your feelings of inadequacy.

There is another reason why you should feel encouraged. Leading a Bible discussion is not difficult if you follow certain guidelines. You don't need to be an expert on the Bible or a trained teacher. The suggestions listed below should enable you to effectively and enjoyably fulfill your role as leader.

Preparing to Lead

1. Ask God to help you understand and apply the passage to your own life. Unless this happens, you will not be prepared to lead others. Pray too for the various members of the group. Ask God to give you an enjoyable and profitable time together studying his Word.

2. As you begin each study, read and reread the assigned Bible passage to familiarize yourself with what the author is saying. In the case of book studies, you may want to read through the entire book prior to the first study. This will give you a helpful overview of its contents.

3. This study guide is based on the New International Version of the Bible. It will help you and the group if you use this translation as the basis for your study and discussion. Encourage others to use the NIV also, but allow them the freedom to use whatever translation they prefer.

4. Carefully work through each question in the study. Spend time in meditation and reflection as you formulate your answers.

5. Write your answers in the space provided in the study guide. This will help you to express your understanding of the passage clearly.

6. It might help you to have a Bible dictionary handy. Use it to look up any unfamiliar words, names or places. (For additional help on how to study a passage, see chapter five of *Leading Bible Discussions*, SU).

7. Once you have finished your own study of the passage, familiarize yourself with the leader's notes for the study you are leading. These are designed to help you in several ways. First, they tell you the purpose the study guide author had in mind while writing the study. Take time to think through how the study questions work together to accomplish that purpose. Second, the notes provide you with additional background information or comments on some of the questions. This information can be useful if people have difficulty understanding or answering a question. Third, the leader's notes can alert you to potential problems you may encounter during the study.

8. If you wish to remind yourself of anything mentioned in the leader's notes, make a note to yourself below that question in the study.

Leading the Study

1. Begin the study on time. Unless you are leading an evangelistic Bible study, open with prayer, asking God to help you to understand and apply the passage.

2. Be sure that everyone in your group has a study guide. Encourage them to prepare beforehand for each discussion by working through the questions in the guide.

3. At the beginning of your first time together, explain that these studies are meant to be discussions not lectures. Encourage the members of the group to participate. However, do not put pressure on those who may be hesitant to speak during the first few sessions.

4. Read the introductory paragraph at the beginning of the discussion. This will orient the group to the passage being studied.

5. Read the passage aloud if you are studying one chapter or less. You may choose to do this yourself, or someone else may read if he or she has been asked to do so prior to the study. Longer passages may occasionally be read in parts at different times during the study. Some studies may cover several chapters. In such cases reading aloud would probably take too much time, so the group members should simply read the assigned passages prior to the study.

6. As you begin to ask the questions in the guide, keep several things in mind. First, the questions are designed to be used just as they are written. If you wish, you may simply read them aloud to the group. Or you may prefer to express them in your own words. However, unnecessary rewording of the questions is not recommended.

Second, the questions are intended to guide the group toward understanding and applying the *main idea* of the passage. The author of the guide has stated his or her view of this central idea in the *purpose* of the study in the leader's notes. You should try to understand how the passage expresses this idea and how the study questions work together to lead the group in that direction.

There may be times when it is appropriate to deviate from the study guide. For example, a question may have already been answered. If so, move on to the next question. Or someone may raise an important question not covered in the guide. Take time to discuss it! The important thing is to use discretion. There may be many routes you can travel to reach the goal of the study. But the easiest route is usually the one the author has suggested.

7. Avoid answering your own questions. If necessary, repeat or rephrase them until they are clearly understood. An eager group quickly becomes passive and silent if they think the leader will do most of the talking.

8. Don't be afraid of silence. People may need time to think about the question before formulating their answers.

9. Don't be content with just one answer. Ask, "What do the rest of you think?" or "Anything else?" until several people have given answers to the question.

10. Acknowledge all contributions. Try to be affirming whenever possible. Never reject an answer. If it is clearly wrong, ask, "Which verse led you to that conclusion?" or again, "What do the rest of you think?"

11. Don't expect every answer to be addressed to you, even though this will probably happen at first. As group members become more at ease, they will begin to truly interact with each other. This is one sign of a healthy discussion.

12. Don't be afraid of controversy. It can be very stimulating. If you don't resolve an issue completely, don't be frustrated. Move on and keep it in mind for later. A subsequent study may solve the problem.

13. Stick to the passage under consideration. It should be the source for answering the questions. Discourage the group from unnecessary cross-referencing. Likewise, stick to the subject and avoid going off on tangents.

14. Periodically summarize what the *group* has said about the passage. This helps to draw together the various ideas mentioned and gives continuity to the study. But don't preach.

15. Conclude your time together with conversational prayer. Be sure to ask God's help to apply those things which you learned in the study.

16. End on time.

Many more suggestions and helps are found in *Leading Bible Discussions* (SU). Reading and studying through that would be well worth your time.

Components of Small Groups

A healthy small group should do more than study the Bible. There are four components you should consider as you structure your time together.

Nurture. Being a part of a small group should be a nurturing and edifying experience. You should grow in your knowledge and love of God and each other. If we are to properly love God, we must know and keep his commandments (Jn 14:15). That is why Bible study should be a foundational part of your small group. But you can be nurtured by other things as well. You can memorize Scripture, read and discuss a book, or occasionally listen to a tape of a good speaker.

Community. Most people have a need for close friendships. Your small group can be an excellent place to cultivate such relationships. Allow time for informal interaction before and after the study. Have a time of sharing during the meeting. Do fun things together as a group, such as a potluck supper or a picnic. Have someone bring refreshments to the meeting. Be creative!

Worship. A portion of your time together can be spent in worship and prayer. Praise God together for who he is. Thank him for what he has done and is doing in your lives and in the world. Pray for each other's needs. Ask God to help you to apply what you have learned. Sing hymns together.

Mission. Many small groups decide to work together in some form of outreach. This can be a practical way of applying what you have learned. You can host a series of evangelistic discussions for your friends or neighbors. You can visit people at a home for the elderly. Help a widow with cleaning or repair jobs around her home. Such projects can have a transforming influence on your group.

For a detailed discussion of the nature and function of small groups, read *Small Group Leaders' Handbook* (IVP) or *Good Things Come in Small Groups* (SU).

Study 1. Believers in a Hostile City. Acts 17:1-15

Purpose: To provide encouragement for Christians in facing challenges they do not feel prepared for.

Question 1. Almost every study begins with an "approach" question, which is meant to be asked before the passage is read. These are important for several reasons.

First, they help the group to warm up to each other. No matter how well a group may know each other or how comfortable they may be with each other, there is always a stiffness that needs to be overcome before people will begin to talk openly. A good question will break the ice.

Second, approach questions get people thinking along the lines of the topic of the study. Most people will have lots of different things going on in their minds (dinner, an important meeting coming up, how to get the car fixed) that will have nothing to do with the study. A creative question will get their attention and draw them into the discussion.

Third, approach questions can reveal where our thoughts or feelings need to be transformed by Scripture. This is why it is especially important not to read the passage before the approach question is asked. The passage will tend to color the honest reactions people would otherwise give because they are of course supposed to think the way the Bible does. Giving honest responses to various issues before they find out what the Bible says may help them to see where their thoughts or attitudes need to be changed.

Question 2. It was Paul's regular practice upon entering a new city, to go to the synagogue and preach. Here he was able to convince some Jewish listeners to follow Christ. However, the majority of his converts were Gentiles who worshiped in the synagogue and believed in God. Among these were a number of highly respected women—probably wives of the principal citizens. It would have been very natural for the

Jews to fear that they were losing influence over these people and so resent Paul for "stealing" them.

Question 3. One of the reasons that Acts was written was to demonstrate that the Christians were good citizens. Although they called Christ their king and refused to worship Caesar, this didn't mean that they were trying to overthrow the government. There did seem to be trouble (and even riots) wherever Paul preached, but Paul wasn't the one inciting these uprisings.

Question 7. The Jews in Thessalonica rejected Christianity without ever taking the time to examine it. The Bereans, while not immediately committing themselves, were willing to give it careful consideration. The Bereans were eager for Scripture study, but the Thessalonian Jews did all they could to disrupt it.

Question 10. This question and the following one can build the group's expectations for what they will find in 1 and 2 Thessalonians. Be sensitive to members who are ready to express a need which they hope this study will answer.

Study 2. Faith That Shows. 1 Thessalonians 1:1-10.

Purpose: To help group members find ways in which their faith can impact others.

Question 3. Perhaps the following definitions will help your group understand what Paul saw:

☐ *Faith* is a trust in God which shows itself in obedient commitment.

☐ *Love* is unselfish care for someone. "Labor of love" expresses the cost of their love, not its result.

☐ *Hope* is an active constancy in the face of difficulties.

Question 5. It is noteworthy that in the same sentence Paul can speak of both the Thessalonians' suffering and joy (v. 6). Although this church faced opposition from the very beginning, the Holy Spirit filled it with a serenity which the world could neither give nor take away.

Question 7. It will probably be helpful to quickly review the activities of Paul, Silas and Timothy from Study 1. Paul is asking the Thessalonians to imitate the way in which he imitates Christ.

Question 9. Your group will probably notice that the Thessalonians' faith became the talk of Macedonia and Achaia. What they may not notice at first is that their faith also caused them to "wait for his [God's] Son from heaven" (v. 10). The point is that the present behavior of the Thessalonians was determined by their firm expectation of what would happen in the future.

Question 11. You may need to remind your group of what you learned about the Thessalonian church in the last study.

Study 3. Gentle Evangelism. 1 Thessalonians 2:1-16.

Purpose: To encourage group members to share their faith with others.

Question 2. Just before coming to Thessalonica, Paul and Silas had been publicly whipped, beaten and then imprisoned for preaching the gospel in Philippi (Acts 16).

Question 5. Paul's concern for these people goes beyond ordinary interest. It included spiritual feeding, delight in their growth, twenty-four hour availability, and the willingness to bear hardship for them.

Question 7. The Thessalonian church was apparently hearing real accusations that Paul was only trying to fleece the public. In response, Paul asks the people to look at his record. Although none of us is perfect (not even Paul), we must at least be sure that we are not using people or preaching one thing while living another.

Question 9. We do not know the exact details of the suffering which Christians faced in Judea, but they must have been well known throughout the Christian church. We do know that in Judea Jesus was crucified; Stephen was stoned (Acts 7), and a persecution forced Christians to scatter (Acts 8).

Question 10. He encourages them by again assuring them of the truth of their message, by reminding them of others who have gone through the same difficulties, and by prophesying the eventual end of their antagonists.

Study 4. Unmistakable Love. 1 Thessalonians 2:17—3:13.

Purpose: To help group members find opportunities to show love through their church or fellowship group.

Question 3. In 2:18 and 3:5 Paul speaks in the first person. He is using the Greek emphatic pronoun to show his deep concern.

Question 5. The trials which Paul refers to in 3:3 are the same trials which began in Acts 17 and are still continuing. The Thessalonian Christians had to contend both with the intolerance of the Gentiles and the jealousy of the Jews.

Question 6. Paul's repeated warnings to the Thessalonians had been much more than just predictions. He had told them that they were "destined" for trials (v. 3).

> Tribulation is not to be wondered at by Christian people as though some strange and unusual thing befell them. Under the conditions of this world, with so many opposed to the gospel, tribulation is inevitable. Human nature being what it is, there are some things we will only learn the hard way. . . . There are qualities of character that are only brought out by affliction. In our hour of need, someone who has these qualities is invaluable. Suffering, then, is part of the very process of living out the Christian life, and we should not regard it as something strange and alien." (Leon Morris, *The First and Second Epistles,* p. 102.)

Question 9. Paul's concern for the Thessalonians is so deep and his life so interwoven with theirs that a good report means he can "really live" (3:8).

Study 5. A Life That Pleases God. 1 Thessalonians 4:1-12.

Purpose: To show group members how they can please God through sexual purity, brotherly love and honest labor.

Question 2. The first-century Greeks only lightly condemned sexual sin. It was taken for granted that the men would have premarital and extramarital affairs. Since the Christians had come from this cultural background, sexual sin probably remained a temptation in which most of their neighbors were indulging.

Question 4. The Greek word which is translated here as "sexual immorality" (v. 3) refers to all sexual intercourse outside of marriage.

Question 6. Paul has not changed the subject in verse 6. "In this matter" refers to the matter of sexual immorality and control. Leon Morris states, "Sexual looseness represents an act of injustice to someone other than the two parties concerned. Adultery is an obvious violation of the rights of another. But promiscuity before marriage represents the robbing of the other of that virginity which ought to be brought to marriage. The future partner of such a one has been defrauded." (Leon Morris, *The First and Second Epistles,* p. 126.)

Question 9. Evidently this was a continuing problem because Paul addresses it again in 2 Thessalonians 3:6-12. What probably happened is that some members of the church believed that since Jesus would soon be returning, there was no point in working or providing for the future.

Study 6. The Hope of Christ's Coming. 1 Thessalonians 4:13— 5:11.

Purpose: To answer fears that group members might have concerning Christ's coming and to help them prepare for it.

Question 3. In verse 15, Paul states that this sequence of events is "according to the Lord's own word." Unfortunately, we have no account of Christ saying anything like this. Probably Paul is referring to an oral teaching of Christ that was not recorded in the Gospels.

Someone may ask, "If the dead in Christ will rise on the last day, where are they now?" As soon as we die, our spirits join Christ in heaven. However, it is not until the resurrection on the last day that spirits and bodies are reunited.

Question 4. The Thessalonians were expecting Christ to return during their lifetime. Therefore, when one of their members died, they were perplexed. Paul reassures them by teaching that even those who die will not miss out on the events of Christ's coming and that all Christians will live forever with the Lord.

Question 5. "The day of the Lord" is a phrase used by the Old Testament prophets to signify the future date on which God would act in power to establish his will. New Testament writers used it in referring to the Last Day.

Question 6. "A thief in the night" expresses the unexpectedness of the event as well as an element of unwelcomeness for those who are not prepared. "Labor pains" is used in the Bible to "express the sheer pain and agony of unpleasant experiences." (I. Howard Marshall, *1 and 2 Thessalonians*, The New Century Bible Commentary [Marshall, Morgan & Scott, 1983], pp. 133-134.)

Question 8. Verses 6 and 7 point out that there are certain kinds of behavior which are appropriate for the sons of night but not for the Christian. The kind of sleep which Paul is talking about here is a moral sleep in which a person is spiritually unconscious to God. Very possibly he was also speaking of a spiritual drunkenness as well. I. Howard Marshall writes, "Paul would have regarded literal sobriety as an essential aspect of the Christian life but probably this idea is contained within the more general one of a spiritual sobriety which avoids any kind of excess that would stifle sensitivity to God's revelation and purpose." (I. Howard Marshall, *1 and 2 Thessalonians*, p. 137.)

Question 10. An example might be that if we are actively showing love to others, then we will not be tempted to indulge ourselves. If I keep reminding myself of my hope of Christ's return, then I will not be surprised by it.

Study 7. Life Among Friends. 1 Thessalonians 5:12-28.

Purpose: To help your group understand its responsibilities toward other members of the body of Christ.

Question 2. This certainly does not mean that some people are more important to God. Paul is referring here to office bearers in the church such as elders.

Question 4. For Paul, the whole church was to be involved in mutual care and not just a group of leaders. As E. Best cleverly writes, "Paul knows nothing of an inert mass, the congregation, on which the ministry operates" (E. Best, *A Commentary on the First and Second Epistles to the Thessalonians*, Black's New Testament Commentaries [London: A & C Black, 1972], p. 223).

Question 6. In these verses, Paul is calling us to be continually con-
scious of God's presence, our dependence on him, and his desire to
give us good gifts.

Question 7. The Bible speaks of various gifts of the Spirit (Rom 12:6-
8, 1 Cor 12:7-11, 28-30) which have been given for the purpose of
building up the Church. If a congregation is hostile or indifferent
toward any of these gifts, then their practice will indeed be quenched
because those who could exercise them will be reticent to do so. Paul
lays particular emphasis here on the gift of prophecy which can be
defined as "speaking words of encouragement which come from
God." Because of their situation, the Thessalonians would have been
most in need of this gift, but perhaps they were not open to receiving
it.

Question 8. Perhaps the Thessalonians had become indifferent toward prophecy because some of what passed for a message from God
was of little value and may have even been opposed to Christian
teaching. To guard against this, Paul tells them to "test everything."
Unfortunately, Paul does not tell us how this is done, but certainly one
way would be to weigh the prophecy or teaching against scripture.

Study 8. Evidence of Faith. 2 Thessalonians 1:1-12.
Purpose: To assure group members that, in the end, God's justice will
prevail and faithfulness will be worth the cost.

Question 3. Whether persecution causes Christians to grow or fail has
much to do with their attitudes toward it. Paul is famous for seeing
even shipwrecks and prison sentences as opportunities for serving
Christ. Another person experiencing the same circumstances might
instead accuse God of abandoning them.

Questions 4-5. Because of the sentence structure, it is not clear
whether the evidence which Paul sees is the suffering itself or the way
in which the Thessalonians have handled themselves while suffering.
What must be noted, however, is that Paul did not think of suffering
as something to be avoided. In fact, he believed it to be inevitable for
all Christians (1 Thess 3:3). To Paul, suffering was a means God used

to teach valuable lessons. So when Paul saw that the Thessalonians were suffering and were learning from that suffering, he knew that God was working.

Question 6. In discussing this question, you may be asked how a loving God could be so vengeful. I. Howard Marshall gives this answer:

From v. 8 it is clear that the punishment described here is for those who reject the gospel, and the content of the gospel is that "God shows his love for us in that while we were yet sinners Christ died for us" and that "while we were enemies we were reconciled to God by the death of his Son" (Rom. 5:8, 10). The God whom Paul is describing is a God who does offer love and reconciliation to his enemies, but if they refuse this offer and continue in opposition to his goodness and love, then it would seem inevitable that, having refused mercy, they must face justice. Nothing in the New Testament suggests that God's love is indifferent to justice, and that he bestows a free pardon on his enemies at the cost of failing to defend the persecuted against the persecutors. Indeed, it is difficult to see how the ultimate justice of God to those who suffer can be defended in a situation where the persecutor knows that in the end he will be freely forgiven. (I. Howard Marshall, *1 and 2 Thessalonians,* pp. 174-75.)

Questions 7-8. A positive aspect of God's judgment is that those who suffer now will be given relief when Christ returns.

Question 9. When Paul says that he wants the people to be worthy, he does not mean that God's kingdom is something they can earn. When God calls us, we are certainly not worthy. However, he does not want us to remain in that condition. Paul's hope is that once we have been called, we will live the rest of our lives in a manner which is worthy. To do this, we need God's power working in us.

Study 9. Lawlessness on the Loose. 2 Thessalonians 2:1-17.

Purpose: To give group members the assurance that they can be saved and know that God will protect them through the horrors which are to come.

Question 4. The "lawless one" is the same being which 1, 2 and 3 John refer to as the "antichrist" and Revelation 11:7 calls "the beast." The Bible prophesies that this individual will oppose God and claim to be in the place of God. *The New Bible Dictionary* explains: "Paul thinks of the supreme effort of Satan as not in the past, but in the future. He does not think of the world as gradually evolving into a perfect state, but of evil as continuing right up till the last time. Then evil will make its greatest challenge to good, and this challenge will be led by the mysterious figure who owes his power to Satan, and who is the instrument of Satan's culminating challenge to the things of God" (L. L. Morris in *The New Bible Dictionary*, J. D. Douglas, ed. [IVP, 1982, p.40).

Question 5. Many guesses have been made as to what is holding back the lawless one. Among the most widely held ideas are the Roman Empire, missionary preaching, the principle of order, and God himself (perhaps through the person of the Holy Spirit).

Question 6. Paul does not mean simply that evil is at work. That has always been true. He is talking here of a special form of evil which is hostile to all that Christ stands for. 1 John 4:3 is speaking of the same thing when it refers to "the spirit of the antichrist."

Question 7. Leon Morris describes it this way: "God is using the very evil that men and Satan produce for the working out of his purpose. They think that they are acting in defiance of Him. But in the end they find that those very acts in which they expressed their defiance were the vehicle of their punishment. Paul has the same truth in other places. For example, in Rom. 1:26 God gave up certain sinners 'unto vile passions.' They thought that they were enjoying their sinful pleasures. They turned out to be 'receiving in themselves that recompense of their error which was due.' The same truth is found in other parts of the Bible also. God is sovereign. No forces of evil, not Satan himself, nor his Man of Lawlessness can resist His might. He chooses to use men's sin as the way in which he works out their punishment" (Leon Morris, *The First and Second Epistles*, p. 234).

Question 9. God will spare us through our total dedication to the truth. Verse 10 says that it is those who refused to love the truth who will be fooled. Verse 12 says that those who don't believe the truth will be condemned. Verse 13 says that the Thessalonian Christians will be spared because they have believed the truth. The truth which Paul refers to is the teaching of the early church which is now contained in the Bible.

Study 10. Lazy Christians. 2 Thessalonians 3:1-18.

Purpose: To help group members see the negative effects that laziness can have on a Christian community and to encourage them to take on their share of the load.

Question 5. Certain members of the church had apparently quit working and were now relying on the generosity of others for support. It is speculated that the reason for doing this was the expectation that Christ would soon return, making it pointless to prepare for the future here on earth.

Question 6. An example might be a family who chooses to attend the church with the best youth program for their children but is not willing to help the leaders in any way.

Question 7. The idea of sacrifice is important to this question. Although by rights Paul did not have to work two jobs, he did in order to avoid every appearance of freeloading on others. He was willing to give up what was rightfully his in order to earn the right to preach the gospel.

Question 9. The lack of association included the avoidance of common meals, private hospitality in homes, and other occasions where these idlers could continue to sponge off the other members. This was not to be used, however, as a means of expressing personal feelings of enmity. The offender was to still be loved and regarded as a brother or sister. The goal was not to chase people off, but to warn them and bring them back.

Study 11. Turning On the Power. 1 & 2 Thessalonians.

Purpose: To review the major ideas presented in Thessalonians and how they can be applied to real-life situations.

Question 1. Concentrate only on the major themes and try to avoid lengthy discussion as most of these ideas will be brought up later in the study.

Question 2. Your summary should include these points:

☐ It is a message of hope and encouragement for Christians and not despair.

☐ It will include both the living and the dead.

☐ There will never be a time when we are separated from God.

☐ It will come suddenly and unexpectedly.

☐ It will not come until the man of lawlessness has been revealed.

☐ Jesus will overthrow the lawless one.

☐ Unbelievers will be fooled by the lies of the lawless one.

Question 4. You may want to ask group members how Paul would counsel a person who fears nuclear war and how he would define a utopia.

Question 5. Be careful not to simply discuss what is wrong with reincarnation, but also how the Christian view can help a person to face death.

Donald E. Baker is the pastor of Christ Community Church (Reformed Church in America) in Palm Springs, Florida. He is a former InterVarsity staff member and the author of the LifeBuilder Bible Studies Philippians: Jesus Our Joy *and* Joshua: The Power of God's Promises.